For Mum and Dad, consummate activists both.

JNW

To my dad, Walter Rudnicki, a lifelong champion
of social justice, with love and admiration.

RR

Acknowledgments

The illustrations were done with the very much appreciated help of Jayde Tynes, Beth Crichton,
Tansy Rudnicki, Stephanie Crane, Dr. Leslie Oliver, Dr. Henry Bishop, the staff of the Black Cultural Centre,
Bucky Hiltz, Clyde F. Macdonald, Lynn McLean, Glen Walker, and Mark and Kelly Rimmington.
A special thanks to my darling wife, Susan Tooke. RR

•

Groundwood Books / House of Anansi Press
groundwoodbooks.com

We acknowledge for their financial support of our publishing program the Canada Council
for the Arts, the Ontario Arts Council and the Government of Canada.

With the participation of the Government of Canada
Avec la participation du gouvernement du Canada | Canadä

Cataloguing data available from Library and Archives Canada

ISBN 978-1-77306-035-4

The illustrations were painted with acrylic paint on watercolor paper.
Photo page 32 courtesy of Mrs. E. Clyke
Design by Michael Solomon
Printed and bound in China

Viola Desmond Won't Be Budged!

Jody Nyasha Warner

PICTURES BY

Richard Rudnicki

GROUNDWOOD BOOKS
HOUSE OF ANANSI PRESS
TORONTO   BERKELEY

VIOLA DESMOND was one brave woman! Now come on here, listen in close and I'll tell you why.

It was a day with a zing in the air when Viola set out on her way.

She waved to Gladys and Sue-Sue who worked for her at Vi's Studio beauty parlor.

Then she stepped into her car and drove away.

Viola drove those winter wet roads with care.
She had a meeting to attend three towns away.
But guess what? She never made it there.

First she heard a rattle. Then she heard a clunk. And her car began to shake.

Quick, quick, Viola drove into New Glasgow, Nova Scotia, to a garage. The mechanic said it would take some long hours to fix up the car, so Viola made plans to pass the time.

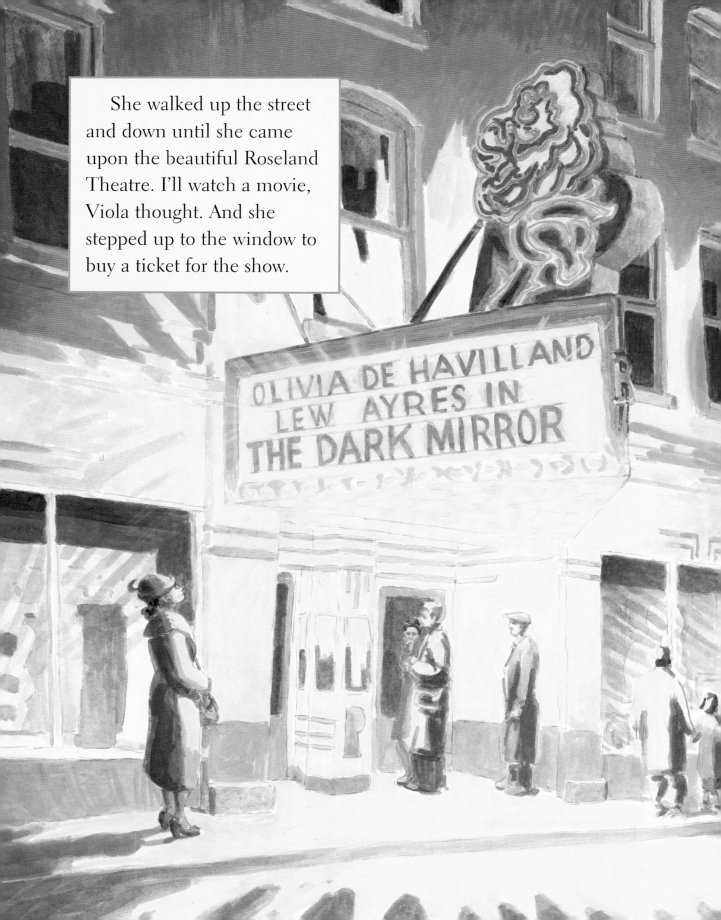

She walked up the street and down until she came upon the beautiful Roseland Theatre. I'll watch a movie, Viola thought. And she stepped up to the window to buy a ticket for the show.

OLIVIA DE HAVILLAND
LEW AYRES IN
THE DARK MIRROR

Her ticket in hand, Viola found the perfect seat, right down close where she could see real good. But then she felt a tap on her shoulder. She looked up into the face of the usher.

"You have a cheap upstairs ticket," she said. "You have to go up to the balcony."

"Well," said Viola, "that cashier must have made a mistake. I'll just go on and buy me a main floor ticket then."

The usher shook her head.

"No. You people have to sit in the upstairs section."

Right then Viola understood crystal clear what she was saying.

It was 1946. Back then the Roseland Theatre, like a lot of other places in Canada, was segregated. That meant black people were not allowed to sit, stand or even be in the same section as white people.

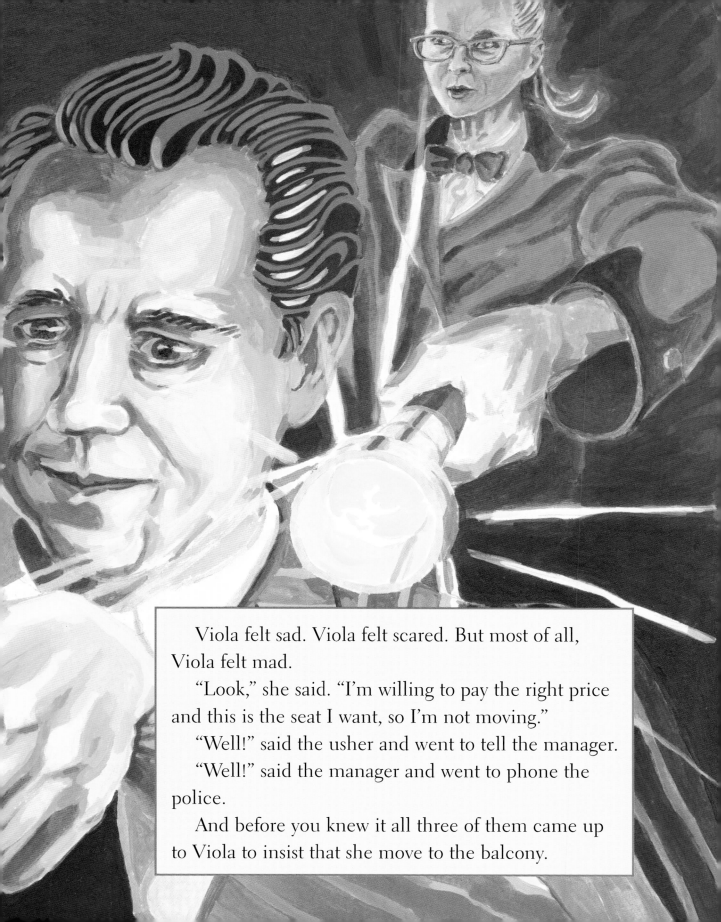

Viola felt sad. Viola felt scared. But most of all, Viola felt mad.

"Look," she said. "I'm willing to pay the right price and this is the seat I want, so I'm not moving."

"Well!" said the usher and went to tell the manager.

"Well!" said the manager and went to phone the police.

And before you knew it all three of them came up to Viola to insist that she move to the balcony.

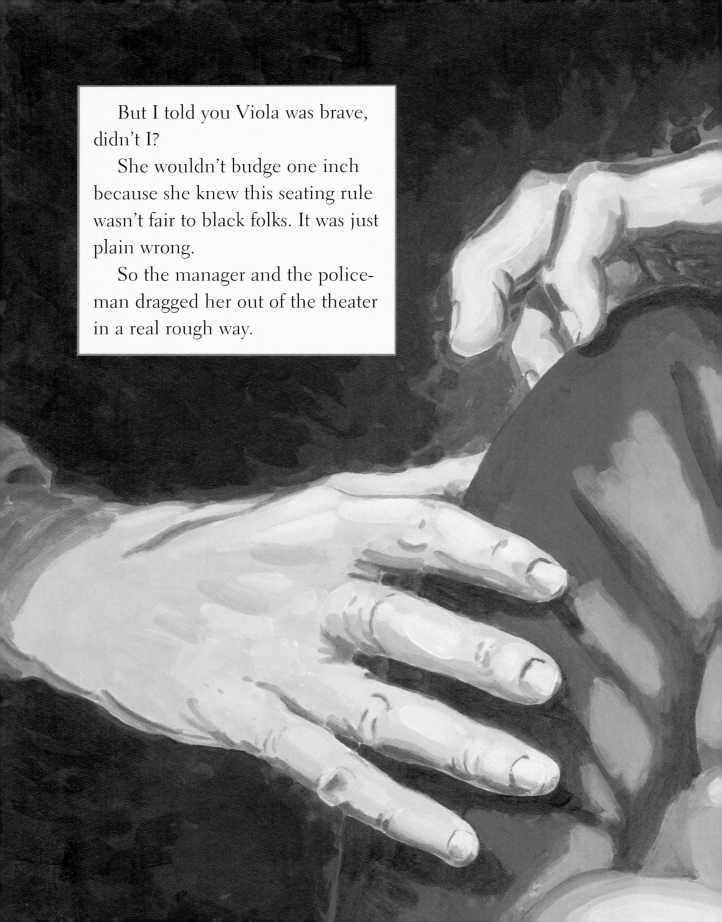

But I told you Viola was brave, didn't I?

She wouldn't budge one inch because she knew this seating rule wasn't fair to black folks. It was just plain wrong.

So the manager and the police-man dragged her out of the theater in a real rough way.

They took Viola to jail.
Can you believe it?
She sat on a hard bench
all night long and tried to
keep her spirits strong.

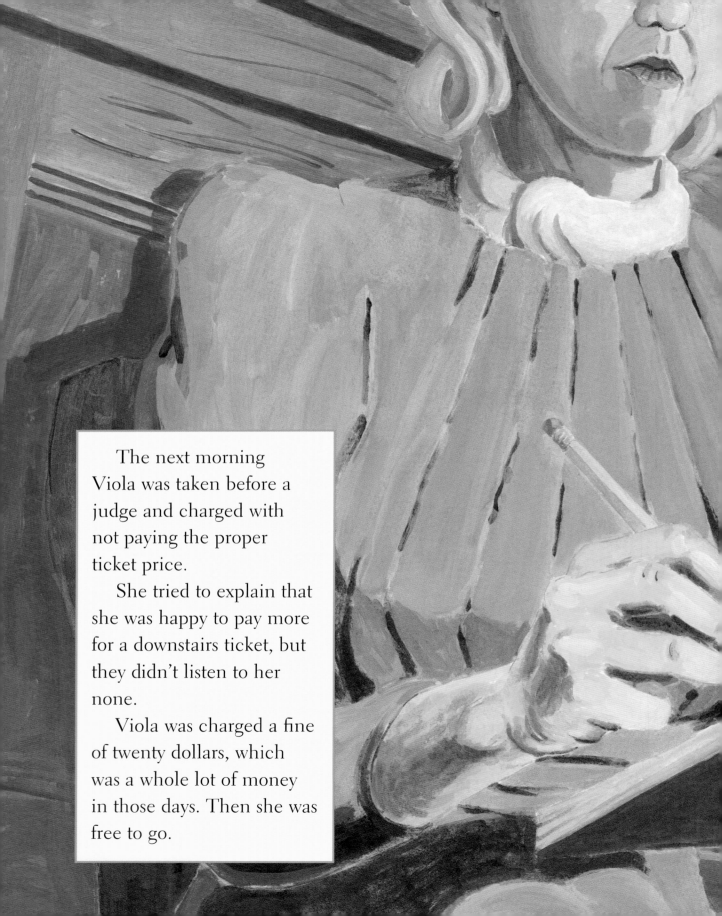

The next morning Viola was taken before a judge and charged with not paying the proper ticket price.

She tried to explain that she was happy to pay more for a downstairs ticket, but they didn't listen to her none.

Viola was charged a fine of twenty dollars, which was a whole lot of money in those days. Then she was free to go.

Viola was glad to get back home to her beauty parlor. When people came by to visit she told them what happened to her in New Glasgow. The story made them angry, too.

So Viola and black community groups in Nova Scotia decided to appeal her charge.

A year later, in 1947, they faced the Nova Scotia Supreme Court. But the judges there sure didn't want to talk about racial segregation. They said Viola's case had been fair, and they canceled her appeal right there.

Still, Viola's bravery made a big difference.

She inspired all kinds of people to fight against segregation, and by the late 1950s it was made against the law.

So come on and join me in saying thank you to Viola Desmond, a real hero, who sat down for her rights.

A Glimpse of African Canadian History

African Canadians have a long history in Canada. The first black person to be documented in the country was Mathieu Da Costa in 1605. Mathieu Da Costa traveled from Europe to Canada to act as a translator between the Mi'kmaq and the French.

Unlike Da Costa, who was a free black man, most other black people in Canada's earliest days were slaves. Slavery was not officially abolished in Canada until 1834, and slaves in Canada had the same kinds of horrible experiences as elsewhere. They could be sold away from family members at public auctions. They were often beaten and were expected to work long, hard hours for no pay. They frequently died young.

When the American Revolution broke out in 1775, the British needed soldiers to fight against the American colonists. They offered black people land and freedom if they would join their army. Many black slaves from the United States did join, and they came to be known as the Black Loyalists. After the war they settled in Nova Scotia, New Brunswick, Ontario and Quebec. Unfortunately many of these Loyalists had to wait years before receiving the land they had been promised, and many more never received it at all. In 1792, disillusioned with Canada, about 1,200 of these Black Loyalists left Nova Scotia and New Brunswick and sailed to Sierra Leone, in West Africa, where they settled.

Another famous group of early African Canadians were the Maroons. They had managed to escape slavery in Jamaica by living, largely hidden, in the hills. In 1796 one group of Maroons called the Trelawny Maroons engaged in a war with the British. When it appeared that neither side would win, they signed a peace treaty. But soon after, the British betrayed the treaty and deported about five hundred men, women and children to Nova Scotia. There the Maroons struggled with the cold weather and faced discrimination from their neighbors. In 1800 almost all of them left for Sierra Leone, where they made their permanent home.

Slavery in the southern United States lasted longer than it did in Canada. From about 1831 to 1865 (when American slavery was abolished) many slaves escaped to freedom in Canada via the famous Underground Railroad. The Underground Railroad was a large network of people who helped slaves escape from their owners and slave hunters. Some provided the fugitives with safe places to stay along the way. Others were "conductors" — people who acted as guides and gave directions on where to go. The most famous conductor was Harriet Tubman, who led dozens of black people to freedom.

There were two other significant waves of early black immigration to Canada. In 1858, when the state of California introduced a tax on African Americans, four hundred black families from San Francisco decided to make Victoria, British Columbia, their new home. And between 1905 and 1911 increasing racism in the United States, along with the promise of cheap land, convinced thousands of black Americans to travel to northern Ontario, Manitoba, Saskatchewan and Alberta, where they became farmers, pioneers and cowboys.

Black people in Canada have often faced discrimination and racism. For instance, from 1912 to 1950, the government actively discouraged black immigration because the white population protested the growing presence of blacks in Canada. During World War I, when blacks signed up to fight on behalf of Canada, they were not allowed to join the white regiments. After two years of protest they formed an all-black battalion. But they were not allowed to fight. Instead they dug trenches and built huts for front-line soldiers.

While Canada never had extensive national laws advocating racial segregation, it was nevertheless widely practiced. It was commonplace for African Canadians not to be allowed to attend the same schools, play on the same sports teams, join the same unions and, in some cases, be in the same public spaces as white Canadians. It is in this context that Viola Desmond, in refusing to move to the black section of a movie theater, challenged segregation in Canada.

Viola Desmond was born in 1914 in Halifax, Nova Scotia. She was a well-respected member of the local black community who owned and operated a popular beauty salon. She also founded the Desmond School of Beauty Culture, since many beauty schools refused to train black students. She was an everyday person who courageously took a stand against racial segregation. When she wouldn't move out of the whites-only section of a movie theater, she was arrested and charged with not paying the additional one cent in tax that a main floor ticket cost. During her trial the courts dealt with the case as if it was a matter of tax evasion — they never admitted it was about a racist seating policy. When Desmond, along with the Nova Scotia Association for the Advancement of Coloured People, tried to appeal her conviction, the case was thrown out of the Nova Scotia Supreme Court on a procedural technicality. Finally, on April 15, 2010, the Nova Scotia government granted Viola Desmond a posthumous Free Pardon, acknowledging that the conviction against her was an error and recognizing her innocence.

Today many African Canadians still experience racism on a daily basis. Viola Desmond continues to be an inspiration for all who choose to struggle against racial discrimination.

Viola Desmond
at sixteen

For more information on African Canadian history see *The Kids Book of Black Canadian History* by Rosemary Sadlier, and *The Underground Railroad: Next Stop, Toronto!* by Adrienne Shadd, Afua Cooper and Karolyn Smardz Frost.